MY FIRST BOOK ABOUT SPACE

A Question and Answer Book

by Dinah L. Moché, Ph.D. • illustrated by R.Z. Whitlock

A GOLDEN BOOK, New York
Western Publishing Company, Inc., Racine, Wisconsin 53404

Copyright © 1982 by Western Publishing Company, Inc. Text copyright © 1982 by Dinah L. Moche. All rights reserved. Printed in the U.S.A. No part of this book may be reproduced or copied in any form without written permission from the publisher. GOLDEN®, GOLDEN® & DESIGN, A GOLDEN LOOK-LOOK® BOOK, and A GOLDEN BOOK® are trademarks of Western Publishing Company, Inc. Library of Congress Catalog Card Number: 80-84783 ISBN 0-307-11870-3/ISBN 0-307-61870-6 (lib. bdg.)

C D E F G H I J

All photographs and artists' conceptions were provided courtesy of the National Aeronautics and Space Administration (NASA) except the painting of the solar system, which was created for this book by Howard S. Friedman.

The author wishes to extend special thanks to Elizabeth K. Rozen, SUNY/Downstate Medical School and Rebecca A. Rozen, Harvard-Radcliffe; Les Gaver, Chief, Audio-Visual Branch, NASA Headquarters, Washington, D.C.; Terry White, Public Information Specialist, NASA Johnson Space Center, Houston, Texas; Frank E. Bristow, Manager, Public Information, NASA Jet Propulsion Laboratory, Pasadena, California; and Janet K. Wolfe, Chief, Educational Services, National Air and Space Museum, Washington, D.C.

What does the world look like from space?

Our world, Earth, is a colorful giant ball. If you look at the earth from a spaceship, you see white clouds, blue oceans, and reddish-brown land. You are too far away to see things like trees, buildings, cars, and people.

Does the earth stand still?

No, but Earth moves so smoothly that you never feel it. The earth is always turning around like a big, slow merry-go-round. It never stops turning. One complete turn takes 24 hours—one day. While the earth turns, it also travels in a gigantic loop around the sun. It goes much faster than the fastest airplane. One trip around the sun takes 365 days—one year.

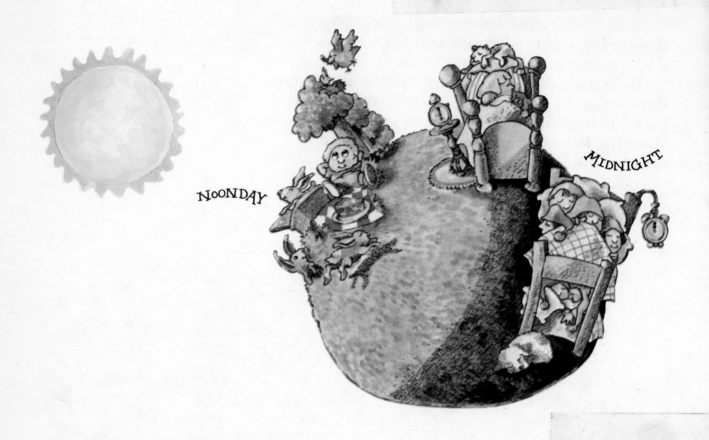

NOONDAY

MIDNIGHT

Why does it get dark at night?

The earth is lit up by the bright shining sun. As your part of Earth turns away from the sun, the sky gets dark. As your part of Earth turns toward the sun, the sky gets light. When your side of the earth has daylight, the other side has dark night. Because the earth is always turning, we always have day and night.

Facts About the Moon

If you walked day and night without stopping to rest, it would take you three months to walk around the moon.

Your weight tells you how hard gravity is pulling on you. The moon's gravity is much weaker than Earth's so you would weigh much less there. If you weigh 60 pounds on Earth, you would weigh only 10 pounds on the moon.

Because of the moon's weak gravity, you could be a champion high jumper there. If you can jump over a wastebasket on Earth, you could leap over a garbage truck on the moon.

Can anybody go to the sun?

No, the sun is much too hot. It is not made of rock
like the earth and the moon. The sun is a gigantic
ball of very hot, shining gases—mostly hydrogen
and helium. Because the gases are so superhot,
no one can even go near the sun.

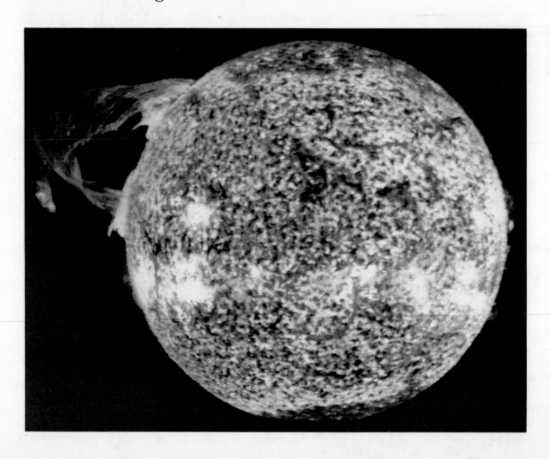

What is the sun?

The sun is a star. Because it is much closer to Earth than any other star, it looks much bigger than the stars you see at night. The sun is 93 million miles away. That may sound very far, but it is just the right distance to give us the light and heat we need to live on Earth.

Warning: Never stare at the sun—even when you are wearing sunglasses. If you do, the sun's rays can blind you.

Facts About the Sun

If you walked day and night without stopping to rest, it would take you 100 years to walk around the sun. Of course, no one can *really* walk on the sun—it is too hot.

← EARTH

It would take more than a million Earths to make a ball as big as the sun. It would take about 109 Earths to make a straight line across the sun.

The sun's gravity is much stronger than Earth's. You would weigh much more there. If you weigh 60 pounds on Earth, you'd weigh 1,680 pounds on the sun.

Why don't we fall off the earth?

Gravity keeps us on the earth. Earth is always pulling everything down toward its center. This pull is called gravity. Gravity holds on to people, houses, oceans, and even the air we breathe. Everything else in space has gravity, too—the sun, the moon, the planets, and all the stars.

Facts About Earth

If you walked day and night without stopping to rest, it would take you a year to walk around the earth.

A spaceship can fly around the earth in just one and a half hours.

You can't see gravity, but you can feel it. Jump! Skip! Hop! Gravity pulls you down every time.

Is there really a man in the moon?

No, although some people think they see a human face when they look at the moon. The moon is made of rock. It is lit up by the sun, but some parts of the moon don't look as bright as others. Certain big dark fields of rock look like two eyes, a nose, and a mouth.

EARTH AS SEEN FROM THE MOON

How far away is the moon?

The moon is our closest neighbor in space. It is
about 240 thousand miles from Earth. Blast off
in a spaceship. In just a few days, you will reach
the moon. The stars you see in the sky at night
are very, very far from Earth. Your spaceship
would take thousands of years to reach one of them.

Does anybody live on the moon?

No. There is no air or water on the moon so there are no plants, animals, or people. Astronauts who traveled to the moon had to take their own air, water, and food with them. They proved that humans can live and work on the moon if they bring their own supplies.

What is the weather like on the moon?

Because there is no air or water on the moon, there
are never any storms or clouds. There is never any
wind or rain. The sky is always clear and dark.
Days on the moon get hotter than boiling water.
Nights get colder than the North Pole.

What is a star?

The stars you see in the night sky are huge,
hot, shining balls of gas like our sun. Stars
look like tiny lights because they are trillions
and trillions of miles away. Some stars are much
bigger than the sun. Giant stars are as big
as a million suns put together.

Do stars shine forever?

No, but most stars shine for billions of years. It takes that long for a star to use up all of its fuel. When stars finally run out of fuel, they die. Some of the biggest stars explode. Others flicker out slowly. Scientists say that the sun, our closest star, will go on shining steadily for at least five billion years.

Facts About Stars

Did you ever try to count the stars? On a clear dark night, you can see about 2,000 of them. There are billions and billions of stars. Most are so far away that you can't see them—even with a telescope.

Long ago, people gave names to groups of stars that look like pictures in the sky. These star pictures are called constellations. One famous constellation is Ursa Major (Big Bear).

PLUTO

NEPTUNE

URANUS

VENUS · MERCURY

JUPITER

THE PLANETS IN OUR SOLAR SYSTEM

What is a planet?

A planet is a world that travels around the sun. Earth
is a planet, and there are eight others that circle
the sun in our solar system. Some of the planets are
smaller than Earth. Others are much bigger. Some are
closer to the sun than Earth. Others are much farther
away. Most of the planets have moons. Earth has one;
Jupiter has many. Planets have no light of their own.
Like Earth, they are lit up by the sun.

Why don't the planets crash into each other?

Each planet stays in its own orbit, or path, as it circles the sun. The orbits are very, very far apart. The planets never move out of their orbits so they never crash into each other. Space probes that go from Earth to Venus and Mars, our closest neighbor planets, have to travel for several months. Space probes that go to the farther planets have to travel for years.

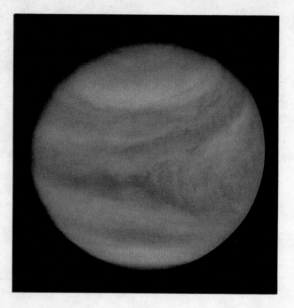

Facts About Planets

Venus is about the same size as
Earth. It is always covered by thick
clouds of poisonous gas.

Mars is called the Red Planet. Space
probes that landed on Mars took
pictures of its surface. Mars has
red dirt and a pink sky.

Jupiter is the biggest planet in our solar system. All the other planets could fit inside gigantic Jupiter. It would take about 10 Jupiters to make a straight line across the sun.

Saturn is famous for the dazzling rings that circle it. The rings are made up of billions of icy particles that go around the planet. Jupiter and Uranus have rings, but theirs are much thinner than Saturn's.

What is an astronaut?

An astronaut is a space explorer. Astronauts
must have many years of special training. They
study the earth and stars from space. They do
experiments to find out how space travel
affects people and materials. Some astronauts
have gone to the moon. Others do experiments
aboard the Space Shuttle.

SPACE SHUTTLE

Are there robots in space?

Yes, although they don't look much like toy robots. Scientists put cameras, computers, and other instruments on robot space probes. They send the robot space probes to places where people can't go yet. The robots take pictures and gather information, which they send back to Earth.

Are there any space creatures?

No one knows yet. Space is huge, and there is still a lot to learn about it. Exploring space is exciting. Maybe one day you will be a space explorer.